CONTENTS

	Page
• Acknowledgements	
• Introduction	
• 'Told by Sheila Hodgetts'	6
• 'Pictured by Edward Jeffrey'	8
• The Publishers & The Books	12
• Rarities	16
• The Collector's Guide	26
• The Collector's Guide part 2	48
• Finding Toby Twirl - Collecting Tips	53
• Other Books by Sheila Hodgetts and Illustrated by Edward Jeffrey	54
• Some Other Books by Sheila Hodgetts	55
• Collector's Book Grading Guide	56

Published by Toby Twirl Ltd
2 Abbots Road, Burghfield Common, Nr Reading,
West Berkshire, RG7 3LD. UK.

ISBN 0-9544720-0-4

Acknowledgements

With very special thanks to the following people for their assistance:

Sheila Hodgetts
Roy Thomas
Carole Ellison
Guy Ellison
Gary & Freda Baker
Martin Hamer
Bob Shepherd
Brian Cotsford
Elaine Gray
Kerry Emmett
Christine Bentley
Bob Taylor
Niki Hayles
Karl Mallard

• • •

**First Published in UK 2003
by Toby Twirl Ltd**
2 Abbots Road, Burghfield Common
Nr Reading, West Berkshire RG7 3LD
Copyright © 2002 Martin Hockley.

Printed and bound in Spain
at Graficas Santamaria S.A., Vitoria
by arrangement with
Associated Agencies Ltd., Kidlington, UK.

Toby Twirl
Adventure Books

Told by SHEILA HODGETTS · Pictured by e. jeffrey

"A Collector's Guide"
by Martin Hockley

Introduction

I was lucky enough to have experienced 'Toby Twirl' as a child growing up in the late 1950's and he was always my particular favourite compared to 'Rupert Bear'. I was fascinated by the stunning artwork produced by Edward Jeffrey.

Unfortunately my original copies did not survive the passage of time in very good condition and when my first grandson was born in 1996, and his parents coincidently decided to name him Toby, I remembered my childhood favourite and following a search of old books stored away in a box I found my only remaining, but tatty, copy. Scanning through it's pages I was instantly transported back to my childhood memories of 'Toby Twirl' and his many adventures, I then decided I would try and complete a 'Toby Twirl' collection for my grandson, well that's my excuse anyway!

I was immediately disappointed at the lack of information available, and at that time only managing to find a couple of copies at what I then thought to be a 'fair' price. I eagerly purchased them and stored these 'finds' away for when my Grandson became older; time passed and with the pressures of working life my search slowed down.

More recently as my eldest grandson approached an age where he would appreciate 'Toby Twirl', and with the help of the Internet, I managed to do much better in locating further copies of these books, however I was still very disappointed with the lack of available information about the Author Sheila Hodgetts, the Illustrator Edward Jeffrey or any details of the publishing run of this fabulous series of books.

As existing collector's are probably already well aware there is very little information available in other publications such as the 'Book and Magazine Collector' catalogue book 'Collecting Children's Books'.

As an avid collector myself I was very keen to see this project through, as I felt this very important series of books really did deserve much better representation in the world of Children's Literature.

These books were so well produced between 1946 and 1958 that 'Toby Twirl' actually gave 'Rupert Bear' a serious rival; not only for the incredible artwork contribution by Edward Jeffrey, which is still used today as an example of illustration to Art Students at Brighton University, but the sheer brilliance of the entire Toby Twirl concept ... so this is not just a Collector's Guide it also serves as a tribute. The 'Toby Twirl' story must be more fully documented.... Hopefully here it is!

Enjoy, and good 'TT' book hunting.

Martin Hockley,
Spring 2003.

The
Toby Twirl
Adventure Books

by
SHEILA HODGETTS

PICTURED BY
e. jeffrey

"A Collector's Guide"
by Martin Hockley

Told by Sheila Hodgetts

The Author of Toby Twirl is Sheila Hodgetts, who was born 27th January 1924 in Laindon, Essex, later moving near to Eastbourne, Sussex where she attended Brighton & Hove High School for Girls as a weekly border.

Sheila joined the WAAF in 1941 and met her husband to be, who was then serving in the RAF. They married in 1942 and have two daughters, Tania born 1945 and Domini born 1948. In 1946, when her husband was demobbed from the RAF,

Sheila Hodgetts circa 1947

the family moved to the West Midlands where they have lived ever since.

Sheila began her writing career in 1943 but her first Toby Twirl book was 'Toby Twirl in Pogland' which was published in 1946. Sheila remembers, when the book was first launched, attending and signing copies in 'Beatties' West Midlands book store, also going to Purnells the printers and watching her books come off the press.

The questions many people had asked were: *What was the inspiration for 'TT'?, Why did the annuals stop in 1958? and Were there any unpublished Toby Twirl books or stories?*

I asked Sheila these questions and here is her answer …

"I always loved Rupert Bear as a child. My father was then the Managing Director of Sampson Low's, and he had the Book Rights of Mary Tourtel's Rupert stories which were published in the Daily Express. After Mary Tourtel died, my father asked me to write something in the same vein to replace them. And so Toby was born. I wrote the stories over the whole period of Toby's publication, and had a job to keep up with the demand. At one time when the newspaper strip was appearing in the Express & Star, the Yorkshire Post and the Manchester Guardian I was actually giving them the scripts over the phone to save time, as we had such a tight deadline. I remember Edward's rough sketches very well, he used to rough them out at the conferences we held in London with the Publishers, when I produced my ideas and plots for future stories, and he roughed out any new characters or scenes which I had in mind. I remember Toby and the Marionette, also the Bullfighter, although I don't think I have a copy of these. But I have Dapple Heath and the Talking Poodle. Dapple Heath 54 was our phone number at the time when I lived between Stafford and Uttoxeter. I know it was at this time that I had the idea for the Sleepy Time Tales which also originally sold for 6d in Woolworth's. Toby was still selling well when they discontinued publication, and I was very sorry about it. But Sampson Low had started publishing Noddy and Sooty, and I think the sheer volume of work must have overwhelmed them. They told me later that it was a big mistake, but I was very busy still with the Sooty books and Sleepy Time Tales, so at the time had little time to grieve. There were no unpublished books, as all the ones I wrote were brought out."

Sheila continues to be pleasantly amazed at the interest in Toby Twirl after such a long time, her greatest interests these days are enjoying her gardening and their eight great-grandchildren.

Pictured by Edward Jeffrey

Self Portrait by Edward Jeffrey - circa 1947
*Picture shows 'EJ' with some of his Toby Twirl characters around him,
reproduced by very kind permission of Edward Jeffrey's family.*

The illustrator of 'Toby Twirl' was Edward Jeffrey, having based Toby on a soft toy that his wife was making at the time, he used his unique drawing skills to bring 'TT' to life. His genius portrayal of movement and attention to detail made the drawings almost move by themselves.

'EJ' was probably the greatest character artist of the 20th century, compare his 'Toby Twirl' artwork to that of 'Rupert' and you will see the difference in detail and depiction of movement. 'EJ' was born on 17th September 1898 and later studied art at Armstrong College, Durham University, Newcastle upon Tyne. He was also a most accomplished landscape painter and exhibited his works at the Royal Institute of Painters in Water Colours, the Royal Society of British Artists, the Royal Welsh Academy, the Royal Scottish Academy, the National Society of Painters, Sculptors and Gravers, and widely in the provinces. Prior to illustrating 'Toby Twirl' 'EJ' had worked for Sampson Low producing a large number of book cover illustrations for various novels, he had also worked on the newspaper strips for 'Rupert' and was the obvious choice of illustrator for TT'. 'EJ's grandson remembers Sheila Hodgetts visiting him at his Yorkshire home studio, and saying that she would prefer a patch on Toby's dungarees to a pocket that 'EJ' had originally drawn. In 1946 'EJ' and his family moved to 'Chantry Studios' Ravenstonedale, Kirkby Stephen, Westmorland (now Cumbria).

R.S. Clarke & Edward Jeffrey c1955

Pictured by Edward Jefferey (continued)

'The Chantry' is where Edward Jeffrey did most of his Toby Twirl illustrations. The family shared the house and studio at this time with R.S. Clark the colour artist who coloured some of the early Toby Twirl work.

'The Chantry' circa 1947

From this studio 'EJ' could see out across the Westmorland countryside and used these views in many of his 'TT' drawings, for example the back-ground scene on the cover of the 1950 TT annual.

'EJ' continued to live and work at Ravenstonedale , moving to 'The Stables' another studio in the village, sometime in the mid 1950's. In later years he would also undertake commercial commissions, despite being almost crippled by arthritis, he painted many 'Pub Signs' for a major brewery, hanging them in the yard of 'The Stables' and painting them from a step ladder, one of his signs can still be seen at 'The Punchbowl' Public House in Underbarrow, Cumbria.

He also designed many greetings cards, often featuring the birds that visited his bird table just outside his studio window. His great love of the Cumbria wildlife, people, landscape and buildings is reflected in his fabulous paint-

'The Stables' circa 1955

ings. His success as a landscape and wild bird painter meant he did many paintings for the card manufacturers 'Valentines' of Dundee, and had submissions selected exclusively for The Queen Mother and The Queen.

'EJ' was also a member of the Lake Artist's Society and the Kendal Art Society, as many as 160 of his colour paintings appeared as cover illustrations for 'Cumbria Magazine' beginning in 1959. His great enjoyment in sketching and painting the Cumbria landscape, particularly it's characteristic features of trees, wildlife, people and buildings, led to his own book 'Edward Jeffrey's Lake District Sketchbook' being published in 1972 by Dalesman Books. His family say that people would visit his studio and buy his paintings off the walls, and when he didn't have any he would hang up his sketches and people would buy them. He was asked to do another painting for The Royal Family, but by that time his wife had died, who had been his life and inspiration, and his hands were so twisted by arthritis that he said he did not want to do a bad painting, despite this he was still painting fabulous pictures and had a book full of commissions when he died in 1978.

The Publishers & The Books

Between 1946 and 1958 The 'Toby Twirl' series of books were published by Sampson Low & Marston, a traditional publishing house established in England circa 1850's and even surviving a German incendiary bomb which totally destroyed their London warehouse in December 1940.

During the period of 'Toby Twirl' publications they were also the publisher for 'Rupert Bear' and the 'Noddy' books amongst a number of others, none of the 'TT' books are marked with a publishing date, as all pre-date ISBN.

These very collectable, approx 10"x 8", hard back 'Toby Twirl' books remain much sought after and are a fabulous insight to a period which now seems sadly long passed in today's much faster world of high technology.

The 'Annuals' were produced each year in time for the Christmas book market, however, as a point of interest, and to avoid any confusion to collectors only the first 'Annual Format' book in 1946 actually bore the title 'The Toby Twirl Annual', this being followed in 1947 by 'The Toby Twirl Story Book' and from 1948 onwards books were published with the title 'Toby Twirl Adventures' or with 'Adventures' forming part of the 'annual's' title. All original 'annuals', 1946 to 1958, have cloth covered spines that vary in colour between red, green or blue.

Just to confuse matters an example of the 1950 annual is shown with a printed laminated spine matching the books gloss boards, (see page 25 in the 'Rarities' section of this book for more details) this being a later reprint by Sampson Low. All of the annuals with a cloth spine originally had an illustrated paper dust wrapper that matched the picture on the book's cover boards. The earliest books are also recognisable by Edward Jeffrey's depiction of Toby with more pointed ears and blue dungarees. Single colour page printing also identifies the first three 'Annuals'. The first fully coloured 'Annual' was published in 1949 with the colour work being done by R. S. Clark who was a friend and professional colleague to Edward Jeffrey. R.S Clark has been credited for colouring further 'Toby Twirl' annuals up to

PICTURED BY e.jeffrey

and including 1953, after which he was dropped by Sampson Low as most of the colour work was being done by Edward Jeffrey anyway.

The Publishers & The Books (continued)

There are three other annual sized hard backed books, and these are the 'Colour Strip Adventure Books', (two featuring three stories each) published in addition to the annuals in 1952 and 1953, plus 'Toby Twirl Dares All Dangers' 1955 (being a reprint of the 1953 'The New Toby Twirl Colour Strip Adventure Book', but this time with only two stories from the original book). These books are thinner editions without cloth spines. They are believed to have been published without matching dust wrappers, and so far I have not seen any examples with them.

In addition to the annual sized books there are eight smaller 5" x 8" hard backed volumes published by Sampson Low between 1949 and 1954, these are the 'Toby Twirl Tales' numbered 1 to 8, each book features two Toby stories. First Editions for Books 1 and 2 from this series are recognisable by not having a red number on the front board or matching dust wrapper.

The 'Toby Twirl Tales' set of books was part of Sampson Low's popular 'Children's Library' that also featured a similar set of 'Noddy' and 'Nicholas Thomas' books. This set is highly collectable and featured here in the 'Collector's Guide Part 2' section of this book.

It would appear today that the demand for 'Toby Twirl' books in general far outweighs their availability, a situation which is set to worsen as more and more people seek to complete their 'Toby Twirl' collections and the new collector's start their own. It's also worth considering that prices are bound to rise over the next few years as general interest in 1950's art is also rising.

The Sampson Low, Marston & Co Ltd Bookstall at the 1951 British Industries Trade Fair.

Photograph reproduced by courtesy of Sheila Hodgetts.

This exhibition stand featured 12 of Sheila Hodgetts books.

Note:
The photograph also shows an advertising statuette figure of 'Toby Twirl with his friend Pete the Penguin', in the top centre back section of the stand, see page 17 for further details of these 'Point of Sale Advertising' figures.

Rarities

Although all 'Toby Twirl' books are now becoming quite rare there are some which are even more difficult to find; interspersed with the 'Annuals' there were a small number of other format publications by Sampson Low these are the 'card' covered large format books, the 6d strip books and the 'Pop-Up' books, all of which were not as hard wearing as the usual board backed 'annuals' or 'Tales', so therefore remain the most difficult to obtain, all of these are featured in the 'Rarities' and 'Collector's Guide' sections of this book.

There are four of the larger format Toby Twirl books, three were produced in the late 1940's and sized 14" x 9" and one early 1950's which is slightly smaller sized 12" x 9", all are richly illustrated in full colour with card covers, each one featuring a single story with a published priced of 2/6d: The first is 1946 'Toby Twirl in Pogland', this also being the very first Toby Twirl book to be published, and was followed in 1947 by 'Toby Twirl Rescues Prince Apricot', in 1948 by 'Toby Twirl and the Mermaid Princess' and in 1952 by 'Toby Twirl and the Magic Ring' (12" x 9").

As a point of interest there are contemporary 'Rupert', and other books, of this same format also published by Sampson Low; two others also by Sheila Hodgetts and illustrated by Edward Jeffrey 'The Sleeping City' and 'One Magic Night' are featured later in this book.

In 1951 LTA Robinson produced the 'Toby Twirl Adventures Painting Book', and in 1952 two Toby Twirl 'Magic' painting books 'Merry Magic' and 'Jolly Magic'.

Two other painting books were published by Samson Low circa 1952; they were 'Toby Twirl's Busy Day' and 'Toby Twirl's Play Day'.

"Toby & His Friend Pete"

*Above: **an extremely rare plaster 'Toby Twirl' Advertising Figure** circa 1951 Approx 15" tall and produced for 'Point of Sale' advertising in book stores. During the height of Toby's success these could be seen in book shops and book departments all over the country, but few have survived.*

Value Guide *in very good condition £250/£300*

Rarities - Toby Twirl in the Newspapers

In March 1950 'Toby Twirl' became a successful newspaper strip appearing in several daily newspapers including The Yorkshire Evening Post; a feature that ran until the end of December 1951, The Wolverhampton Express and Star, The Bolton Journal (4 frames per week), The South Wales Evening Post and Manchester Guardian.

Value Guide for Original Strips £5 each.

Meet Toby's boss

PICTURED here is 26-year-old Sheila Hodgetts, creator of Toby Twirl, a series of whose adventures begins in to-morrow's Evening Post

Mother of two children — Tania (5) and Domini (2)—Sheila lives in the country and has just started a chicken farm. Her father was managing director of a leading book publishing firm, and it was due to him that she first tried her hand at writing six years ago. Since then she has had 12 books published.

Any Yorkshire connections? 'Great-grandfather came from Yorkshire, she says.

There is a close Northern link with Toby Twirl himself, however. Illustrations to the tales are done by Westmorland artist Edward Jeffrey.

The Yorkshire Evening Post
Thursday March 23rd 1950

This article preceded the huge daily following Toby was soon to develop with the launch of his newspaper strip feature, as 'Toby Twirl' became set to follow in the footsteps of 'Rupert' if only for a short while.

Examples of Toby's daily newspaper feature, these taken from The Yorkshire Evening Post, are copies from Edward Jeffrey's own scrapbook:

Below: **Yorkshire Evening Post, 29th May 1950 and 7th August 1950**

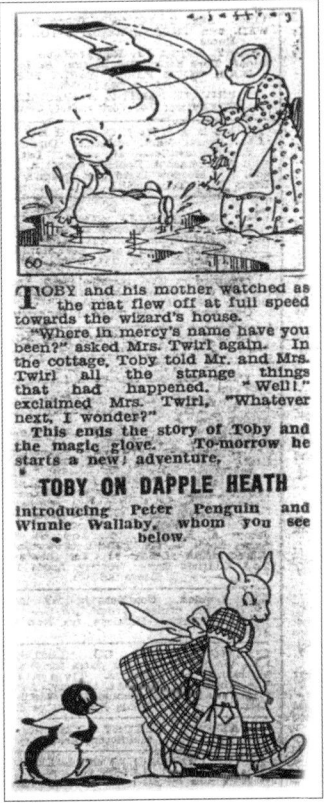

Left: **Edward Jeffrey's own scrapbook containing the complete run of newspaper strips from The Yorkshire Evening Post.**

Rarities - The 6d Strip Books

After the success of the newspaper strips four much smaller, approx 3"x 6", thin card covered 'strip booklets' were on sale at 6d each: 'Toby Twirl On Dapple Heath', 'Toby Twirl and The Talking Poodle', Toby Twirl and The Bull Fighter' and Toby Twirl and The Marionette', these came about following the huge popularity of the various Toby Twirl newspaper strips such as the daily feature in The Yorkshire Evening Post; all Toby Twirl 6d Strip books are now very rare.

c 1954 'Toby Twirl on Dapple Heath', **Value Guide** £30.

c 1954 'TT and The Talking Poodle', **Value Guide** £30.

The other two strip books, 'Toby Twirl and the Bullfighter' and 'Toby Twirl and The Marionette' are extremely rare and their **value guide** would be around £45, but you may have to pay even more if you are lucky enough to find one.

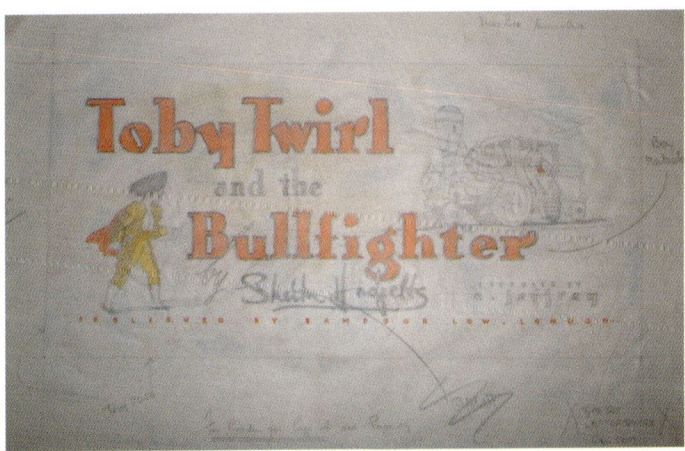

*Above: **Some of the original artwork for 'Toby Twirl and The Bullfighter' reproduced by kind permission of Edward Jeffrey's family.***

Rarities - Painting Books & Jigsaws

It is very difficult to put a price guide on these really rare items as they are so difficult to obtain; they more or less command their own price at whatever the collector is willing to pay for them, a realistic **value guide** would be around £75, however, recent auction prices up to £110 are known to have been paid for such items.

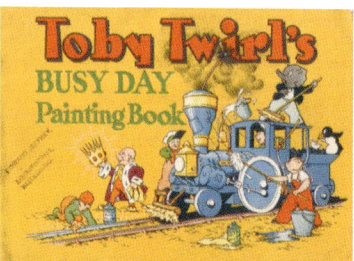
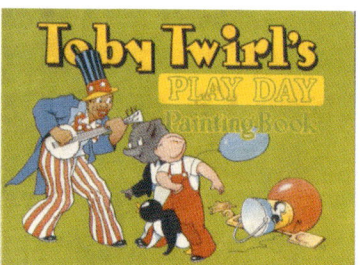

Above: **'Toby Twirl Adventure'** *painting book published by LTA* **Robinson** *1951.*
'Busy Day' *and* **'Play Day'** *circa 1950,* **painting Books** *published by Sampson Low.*

Right: **'Merry Magic'** *1952* **one of two 'magic' painting books published by LTA Robinson, the other title is 'Jolly Magic'**

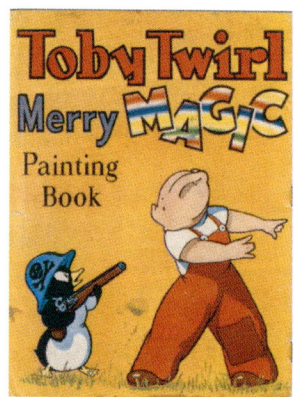

Left:
'Toby And The Dilly-Puff'
Jigsaw box
(5" x 7" x 1")

Above: **'Toby Twirl and the Little Man In Green'** **Jigsaw** *(c1954)*

4th of 4 produced by Sampson Low, box approx' 8" x 6.5" Number of Pieces: 250.

T.101 **Toby Twirl and the Three Princesses**
T.102 **Toby Twirl meets a Knight in Armour**
T.103 **Toby Twirl and the Dilly Paddle**
T.104 **Toby Twirl and the Little Man in Green**

Below**:**
the made-up jigsaw,
comprising of 204 pieces. One of a set of 4 known jigsaws, the bottom of this box lists the 4 jigsaws by title each having over 200 pieces:

1) 'Toby's Car Race'
2) 'Toby Meets A Real Pirate'
3) 'Toby And The Dilly-Puff'
4) Toby In Santa Claus' Toyland'

(all circa 1952)

Original artwork by Edward Jeffrey exists for another 4 jigsaws, together with working titles of 'Train Spotting In DillyLand', 'The Building of Dilly-Town Bridge', 'The Dilly-Paddle Afloat Again' and 'The Dilly-land Air Display', however, it's believed that none of these jigsaw titles were produced.

Rarities - Pop-Up Books

'Toby Twirl's Dilly-Paddle Pop-Up Book',

published circa 1954, approx. 8" x 10" laminated pictorial board covered book. This Pop-Up was published with a red plastic covered wire spiral spine and red end papers, and later with a normal binding without end papers, and features 5 'pop-up' pages, featuring one Story with 18 colour pages, may also have been published without hard covers.

Value Guide £85/£100. First edition.
£75/£95. Other editions.

'Toby Twirl's Pirate Pop-Up Book',

published circa 1955 approx. 9" x 7", is now very hard to find. Featuring 10 colour pages with 3 pop-up pages. As with the thin card covered 'Strip Books' the scarcity of the 'pop-ups' is due partly to the delicate nature of these editions, and the possibility that print runs may have been much lower than for the 'annuals'.

Value Guide £100/£125

Rarities - Others

*This picture (left), despite the obvious damage to the spine cover, clearly shows an **alternative edition to the 1950 annual.** This is believed to be a later reprint, (circa 1956), of the 1950 annual by Sampson Low.*

Only this one example is known featuring a laminated binding matching the books original 1950 dust wrapper, other annuals may also have been re-printed in this format but so far no others have come to light.

Value Guide £40/£45
(with spine cover intact)

*Above Left: **An original 1953 'Printer's Block'** for the story 'Toby Twirl and The Magic Boot', featured in 'The New Toby Twirl Colour Strip Adventure Book', the block is 4" square mounted on a 1" teak wooden block.*

Value Guide £75

*Above Right: **The actual 'block' picture from this story.***

The Collector's Guide

This is the publishing order as I have been able to determine by research and cross-referencing the inscriptions in numerous books including many dated and signed by Edward Jeffrey himself. The following 'value guide' is for books in 'Very Good' (VG) condition, expect to pay at least £10 more for books with good original dust wrappers where available, and up-to a further £15 - £20 more for books in 'Near Fine' (NF) condition. For books in only 'Good' (G) condition deduct 50%. For books in 'Poor' (P) condition deduct 75%.

See page 56 for condition guide details. Edition variations are also featured where known:

1946 *'Toby Twirl In Pogland'*

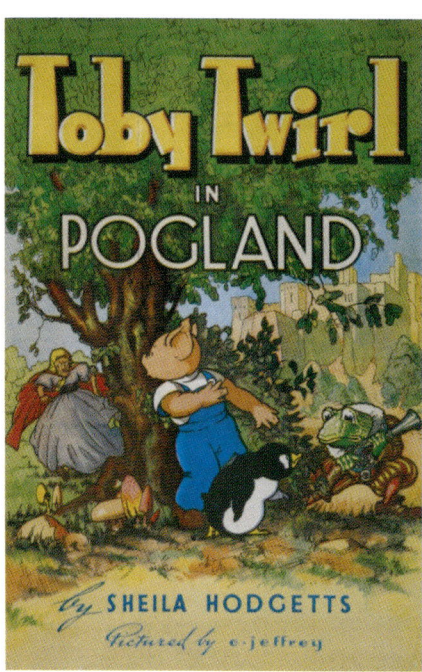

Published price 2/6d, this was the very first Toby Twirl book, a large format card covered book featuring one story with 16 full colour pages, actual Book size is approx 14" x 9". The story tells how Toby rescues Princess Flower from a wicked witch and breaks the spell of sleep which lies over the Kingdom of Pogland. Also featured in this story is when Toby first meets his friend Pete the Penguin.

Value Guide £100/£120

1946 'The Toby Twirl Annual'

The Toby Twirl Annual' published Price 7/6d, first of the 'Annual' Toby Twirl Books. 10" x 8". 123 pages with single colour page printing.. Another early feature of Edward Jeffrey's Toby Twirl character depiction found in this book is his curly, or 'twirly' tail poking through the back of his dungarees, a feature that was dropped from later depictions of Toby.

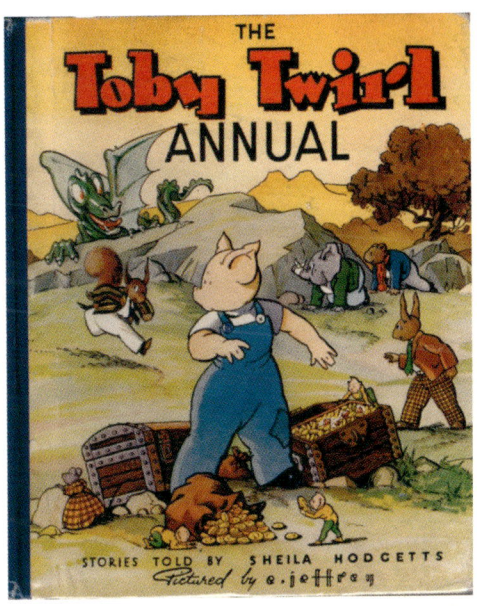

Contents:

Toby Twirl and The Snow Queen
Painting Page
Tohy Twirl at Dragon's Lair
Painting Page
Toby Twirl on Treasure Island
Painting Page

Value Guide £60/£65

1947 *'Toby Twirl Rescues Prince Apricot'*

Published price 2/6d. The second of the large format card covered books featuring one story, with 16 full colour pages, actual Book size 14" x 9".

The story tells how Prince Apricot is held prisoner in an old tower and Toby and Apple Pete attempt to rescue him, they are trapped, but later an Ancient Dame rescues them and casts a spell on their enemy the Earl of Lemon. Toby in return promises to find the Ancient Dames grand-daughter and after many narrow escapes and perilous adventures they free the maiden from the palace of Raj-Pat-U and return to the old tower to deal with the Earl of Lemon.

Value Guide £100/£120.

1947 'The Toby Twirl Story Book'

Published Priced 7/6d The second of the 'Annual' Toby Twirl Books, 10" x 8" - 127 pages with single colour page printing. This Annual seems to be the most commonly available despite it's age; it's lower value is based on availability. Toby is still sporting his blue dungarees on the cover of this book which features four stories plus activity pages.

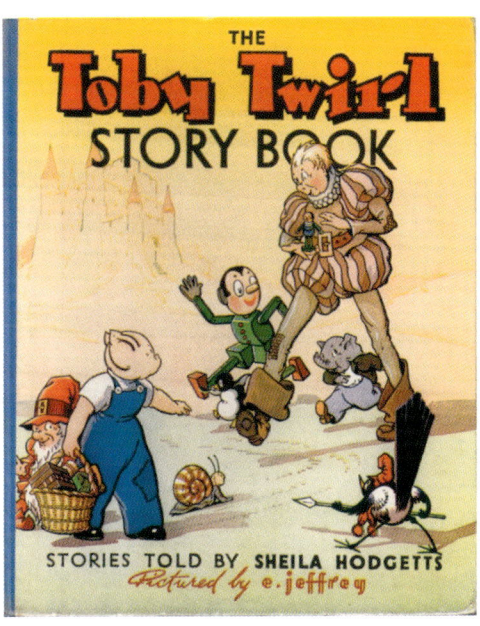

Contents:

Toby Twirl and the Red Gnome
What Has Eli Caught? (Dot to Dot)
Circus Painting Picture
Toby Twirl and the Wooden Prince
Seaside Painting Picture
Blind Man's Buff (Hidden detail)
Toby Twirl's Adventures with Giant Gormless
Toby Twirl's Song
What Did Toby See? (Word Game)
Toby Twirl on the Enchanted Isle
Toby's Lost Cycle (Maze Game)

Value Guide £20/£25.

1948 'Toby Twirl and The Mermaid Princess '

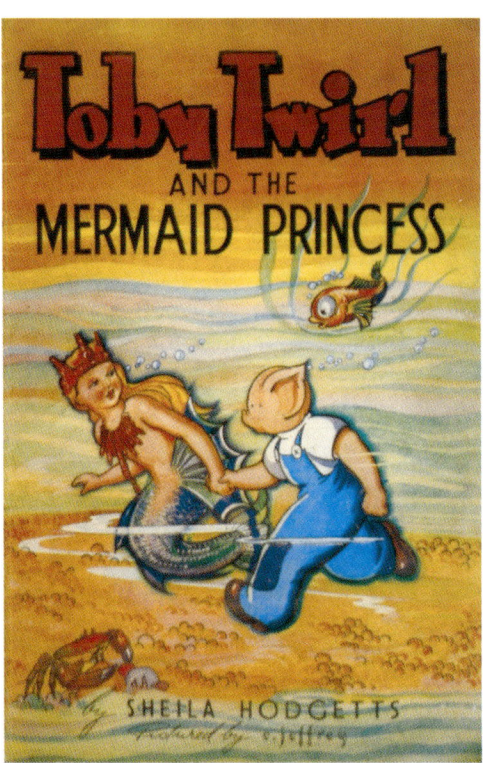

Published price 2/6d. Third of the large format card covered books featuring one story with 16 colour pages, actual book size approx 14" x 9".

The story tells how Toby, whilst fishing with his friend Ben Beaver, finds himself accidentally transported to an underwater Kingdom where he meets the Mermaid Princess and her family. Toby is then invited to visit their underwater Palace but soon learns that her uncle intends to send her away. Toby is informed that only one creature can help, so he sets out and finds the ferocious Tuffin who gives him a magic potion to take back to the Palace and slip into the wicked uncles drink, Toby with the aid of the magic potion rescues the Mermaid Princess from her wicked uncle after he drinks the potion and becomes kind.

Value Guide £100/£120

1948 'Toby Twirl Adventure Stories'

Published Price 7/6d Third of the 'Annual' Toby Twirl Books, 10" x 8" - 127 pages with single colour page printing. Featuring four stories and activity pages, with puzzles being credited to R.S. Clark, who later was to add the colour to many of the Toby Twirl books. The cover of this annual marks the start of the change to Toby's red dungarees.

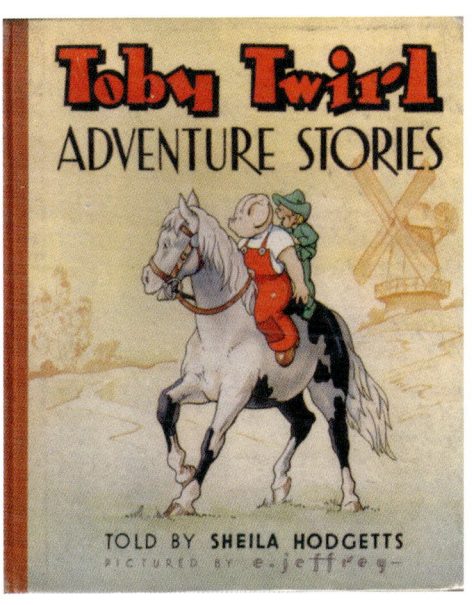

Contents:

Toby Twirl and the Magic Drum
Clown Painting Picture
Toby Is Going Hiking - A Round Game
Toby Twirl and the Dilly-Puff
What Is Wrong With This Picture?
Toy Fair Painting Picture
Toby Twirl and the Piebald Pony
What Is Toby Showing To Peter?
You Can Draw Toby
The 'Adventure' Crossword Puzzle
Toby Twirl and the Christmas Toys
Milkmaid Painting Picture
How Did The Dilly-Puff Get Home? (Maze)

Value Guide £35/£40.

1949 'Toby Twirl Adventures'

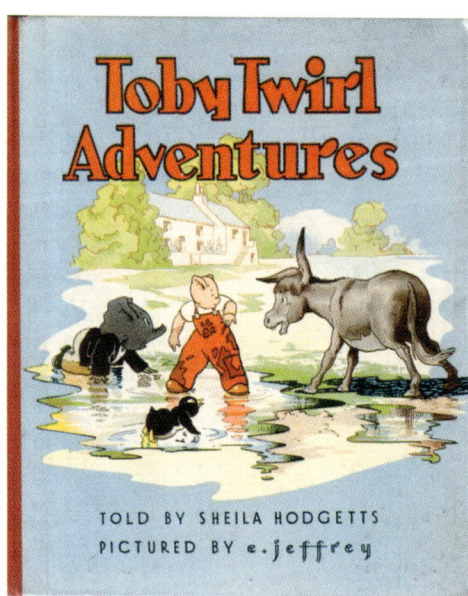

Published Price 7/6d Fourth of the 'Annual' Toby Twirl Books. 10" x 8" - 125 pages and for the first time with full colour page printing. Featuring five stories, with the colour work credited to R. S. Clark. The background cover scene was inspired by the actual landscape around EJ's Studio.

Contents:

View of Long Ripton
Toby Twirl and the Enchanted Swan
An Invitation (Dot to Dot)
Toby Twirl and the Puppets
Noah's Ark Painting Page
Toby Twirl and the Smugglers
Treasure Hunt (Maze puzzle)
Toby Twirl Crossword Puzzle
Toby Twirl's Christmas Adventure
A Round Game- 'The Captain Sails'
Toby Twirl and the Magic Slippers

Value Guide £50/£55

1950 'Toby Twirl Adventures'

Published Price 7/6d . Fifth of the 'Annual' Toby Twirl Books. 10" x 8" 117 pages with full colour page printing.

A bumper packed edition featuring five stories, with the colour work being credited to R. S. Clark. The background cover scene was inspired by the actual landscape around EJ's Studio.

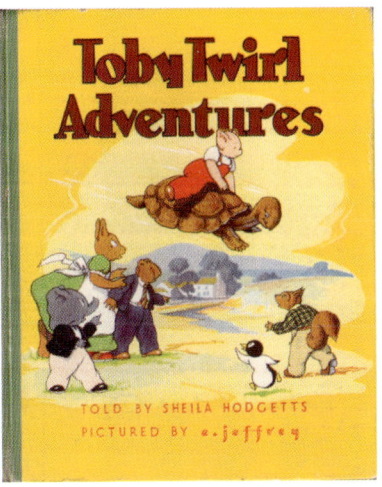

Contents:

Toby Twirl and the Rocking Dragon
Toby's Motor Car - Painting Page
Toby Twirl's River Adventure
Game - "Toby Twirl in the Wild West
Toyshop Memory Game
To the Rescue - Another Dilly-Puff Adventure
Toby Twirl Gets Captured
Mr. Noah's Crossword Elephant
Pete and the Lion
Toby Twirl and the Flying Tortoise
The 'TOBY WORD' Game
Toby Twirl and the Little Chief
The Circus - Painting Page
Toby Twirl Captures Black Benjie
The Gamekeeper Picture Puzzle
How to make Acorn Andy and his Pets

Value Guide £35/£45. *(Also see 'Rarities' page 25).*

1951 'Toby Twirl Adventures'

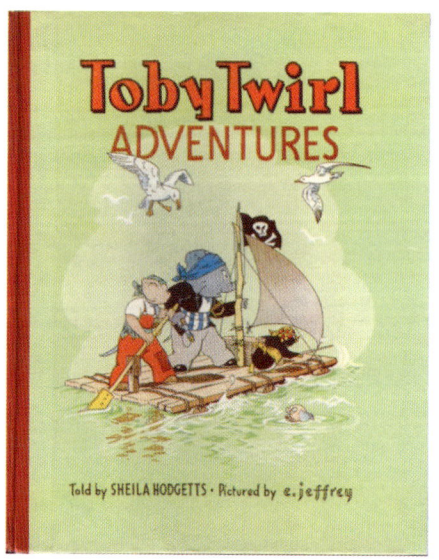

Published Price 7/6d
Sixth of the 'Annual' Toby
Twirl Books. 10" x 8". 92
pages with full colour page
printing.. Featuring
six stories, with the
colour work credited
to R.S. Clark.

Contents:

Toby Twirl and the Enchanted Cottage
How Many Objects: Picture Puzzle
The Lame Reindeer
Toby Twirl and the Crafty Crone
How To Make A Weather Bird
Game: Toby Twirl's Adventures
The Cottage Crossword
Toby, Eli and Pete turn Pirates
Winnie Meets ... Who?: Picture Puzzle
The Kings Treasure Chest
Game: Potato Race
Toby Twirl searches for the Stolen Wand
Toby's Boating Lake: Painting Page

Value Guide £35/£40.

1952 'The Toby Twirl Colour Strip Adventure Book'

Published Price 4/6d.

First of the slimmer hard backed books, this one with matt paper covered panoramic pictorial boards. (Carefully open book out to reveal the full cover picture)

It is possible that this book was published with a matching dust wrapper, however, I have not seen any examples so far.

10" x 8" - 44 pages with full colour printing. Featuring three stories.

Contents:

Toby Twirl and the White Rabbit
Toby Twirl and the Three Dwarfs
Toby Twirl and the Golden Cockatoo

Value Guide £50/£55

1952 'Toby Twirl and The Magic Ring '

Published price 2/6d. Large format card covered book, featuring one story with 14 full colour pages. Actual Book size 12" x 9".

The book is similar in format to the larger card covered books produced in 1946, 1947 and 1948.

The story tells how Toby is taken to a castle by a strange wooden horse, and is put in a dungeon by the wicked king. He escapes and recovers the Magic Ring, and so restores the rightful king to his throne. *This particular book is very difficult to find and will probably prove even harder to find than it's 1940's 'large format' predecessors such as 'Pogland'.*

Value Guide £120/£130

1952 'Toby Twirl Adventures'

Published Price 7/6d
Seventh of the 'Annual'
Toby Twirl Books.10" x 8".
68 pages with full colour
page printing.

Featuring six stories, with
the colour work credited
to R.S. Clark.

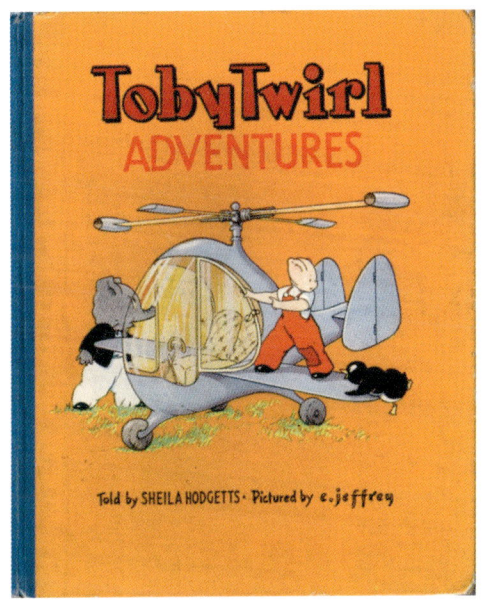

Contents:

Toby Twirl and the Black Stranger
The Fairy Queen's Crown
Eli's Balloon Crossword
Toby Twirl and the Carpet Merchant
In The Valley Of The Dragon
Toby Twirl on Trick Island
Toby Twirl and the Fox
Game: Toby Twirl Adventure

Value Guide £35/£40.

1953 'Toby Twirl Adventures'

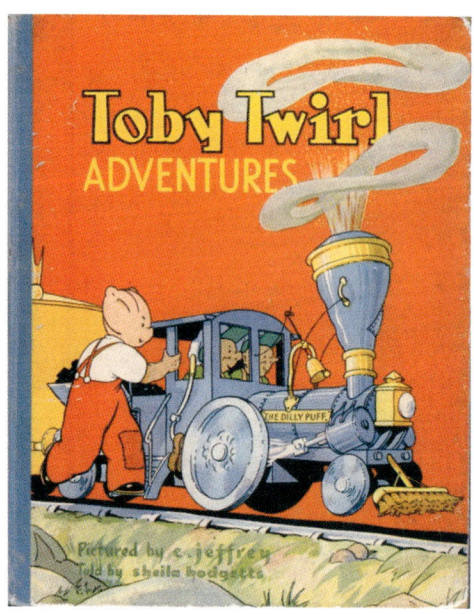

Published Price 7/6d. Eighth of the Annual' Toby Twirl Books.

10" x 8". 68 pages with full colour page printing. Featuring seven stories, with the colour work credited to R.S. Clark.

Contents:

Game: Catch The Leader
Toby Twirl and the Shirt of Mail
The Exciting Picnic
Toby Twirl's Crossword
Toby Twirl and the Ragged Princess
Toby Twirl and the Jungle Boy
Pete in Trouble
The Launching of the Dilly-Paddle
The Little Acrobat
Game: Stop The Road

Value Guide £35/£40.

1953 'The New Toby Twirl Colour Strip Adventure Book'

Published Price 4/6d. Second of the slimmer hard backed books, this time with glossed paper covered panoramic pictorial boards. (Carefully open book out to reveal the full cover picture)

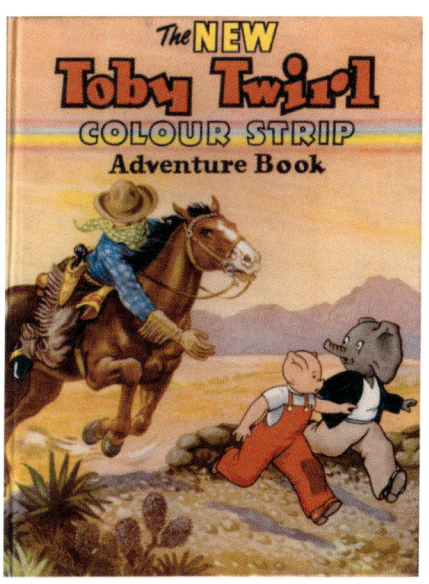

Again it is possible that this book was published with a matching dust wrapper, however, I have not seen any examples so far. According to a very interesting inscription by Edward Jeffrey in a family copy of this book the colour work was not done at his Ravenstonedale 'Chantry Studios'.

10" x 8" - 44 pages with full colour printing. Featuring three stories.

Contents:

Toby Twirl and the Rustlers
Toby Twirl and the Magic Boot
Toby Twirl and the Genie

Value Guide £45/£50

1954 'Toby Twirl Adventures'

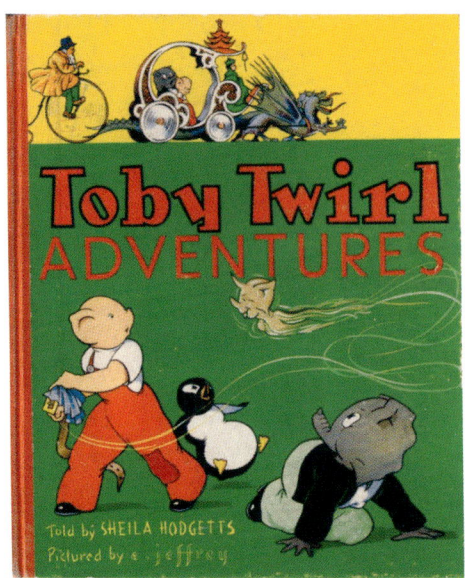

Published Price 7/6d ninth of the 'Annual' Toby Twirl Books. 10" x 8". 76 pages with full colour page printing.

Featuring eight stories.

Contents

Game: Who Can Collect The Most Toys !
Toby Twirl and the Stolen Jewel
Another Dilly-Puff Adventure
A Picture to Paint
Winnie's Cloths Line
Toby Twirl and the Midshipman
Toby's Nature Crossword
Warty Weasel's Trick
Toby Twirl and the Boy King
Another Picture to Paint
Toby Twirl and the Tired Genie
Toby, the Monkey and the Organ Grinder
Game: A Journey Into Bandit Land

Value Guide £50/£55

circa **1954** 'Toby Twirl Adventures'

Published Price 7/6d
Cover Variation of:
ninth 'Annual' Toby Twirl
Book. 10" x 8".
76 pages with full
colour page printing.

Featuring eight stories.

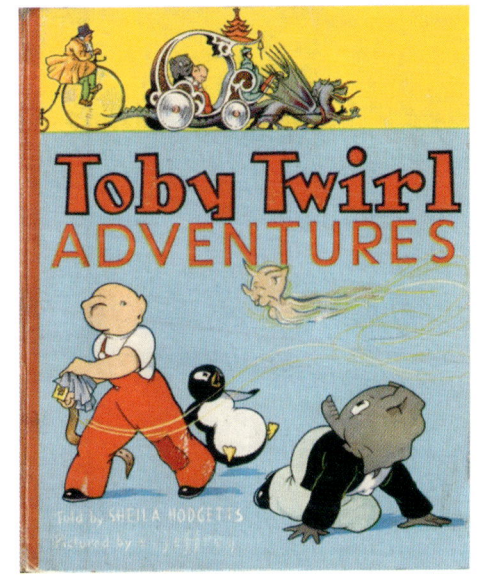

Contents (same):

Game: Who Can Collect The Most Toys !
Toby Twirl and the Stolen Jewel
Another Dilly-Puff Adventure
A Picture to Paint
Winnie's Cloths Line
Toby Twirl and the Midshipman
Toby's Nature Crossword
Warty Weasel's Trick
Toby Twirl and the Boy King
Another Picture to Paint
Toby Twirl and the Tired Genie
Toby, the Monkey and the Organ Grinder
Game: A Journey Into Bandit Land

Value Guide £40/£45

1955 'Toby Twirl Adventures'

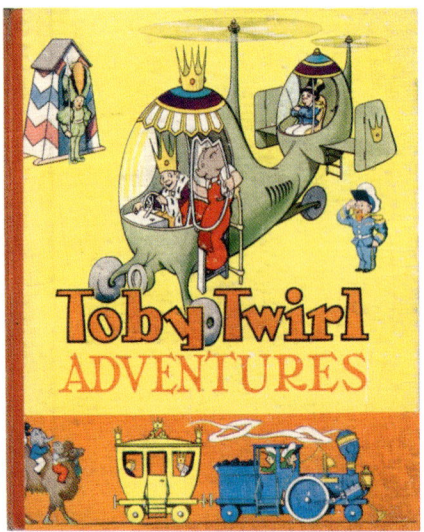

Published Price 7/6d Tenth of the 'Annual' Toby Twirl Books. 10" x 8". 76 pages with full colour page printing throughout, packed with activity pages and featuring six stories.

Repeated story or feature from 1951 annual.

Contents:

Game: Let Us All Go Sledging !
The Mystery of the Dilly-Puff Drivers
A Picture to Paint - Bonfire Night
Game: Toby Twirl's Adventures *
Game: Toby 's Mystery Trip
Game: How Many Objects ? *
The Lame Reindeer *
Toby Twirl and the Crafty Crone *
Game: Some of Toby's Adventures
Toby, Eli, and Pete Turn Pirates *
The King's Treasure Chest *
Game: Potato Race
Toby Twirl's Balloon Trip
Game: Who Wants A Car ?
Game: Whoopee ! Here's Treasure Trove !

Value Guide £45/£50

1955 'Toby Twirl Dares All Dangers'

Published Price 4/6d.

This edition is a partly repub-
lished version of the 1953
'The New Toby Twirl Colour
Strip Adventure Book' (Second of the slimmer hard
backed books). The only
difference being the matt
paper covered (unlaminated)
boards, with only the first
two stories, blank end papers and a new cover title.

(Carefully open book out to
reveal the full cover picture)

Again it is possible that this
book was published with a matching dust wrapper, however, I
have not seen any examples so far.

10" x 8" - 44 pages with full colour printing. Featuring two
stories.

Contents:

Toby Twirl and the Rustlers
Toby Twirl and the Magic Boot

Value Guide £40/£45

1956 'Toby's New Adventures'

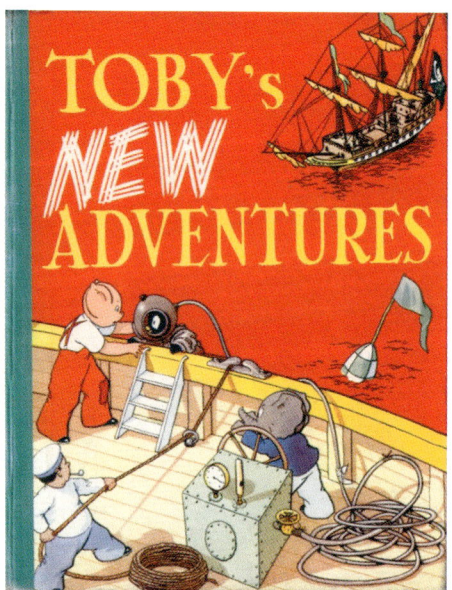

Published Price 7/6d eleventh of the 'Annual' Toby Twirl Books.

10" x 8". 76 pages this time with a mixture of full colour and single colour page printing. Featuring four stories.

This was the first time 'Twirl' did not appear in the title, which may be an indication of the popularity 'TT' had gained by 1956, although his full title was reinstated in time for the next annual.

Contents:

Picture: Hurrah for the 'Dilly Paddle'
The Lost Silver Bars
Toby Twirl and the Magic Glove
Toby Twirl and the Prince with the Tail
Toby Twirl and the Magic Forest

Value Guide £40/£45.

1957 'Toby Twirl Adventures'

Published Price 7/6d.
Twelfth of the 'annual' Toby
Twirl Books and a re-issue
with new cover of the tenth
of the 'Annual' Toby Twirl
Books

10" x 8" - 76 pages with full
colour page printing Back
cover illustration for both
1955 and 1957 editions are
similar.

*Repeated story or feature
from 1951 annual.*

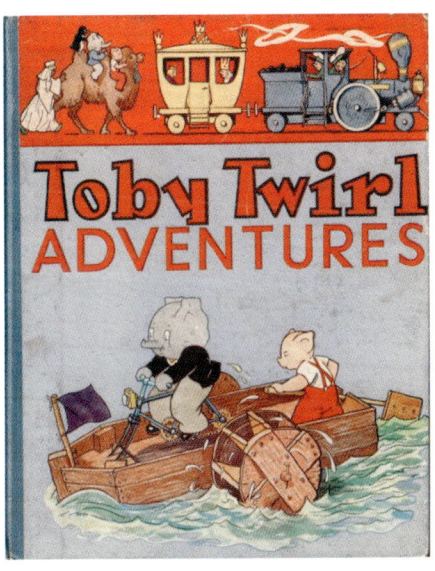

Contents (same as 1955):

Game: Let Us All Go Sledging !
The Mystery of the Dilly-Puff Drivers
A Picture to Paint - Bonfire Night
*Game: Toby Twirl's Adventures **
Game: Toby 's Mystery Trip
*Game: How Many Objects ? **
*The Lame Reindeer**
*Toby Twirl and the Crafty Crone **
Game: Some of Toby's Adventures
*Toby, Eli, and Pete Turn Pirates **
*The King's Treasure Chest **
Game: Potato Race
Toby Twirl's Balloon Trip
Game: Who Wants A Car ?
Game: Whoopee ! Here's Treasure Trove !

Value Guide £50 / £55

1958 'Toby Twirl Adventures'

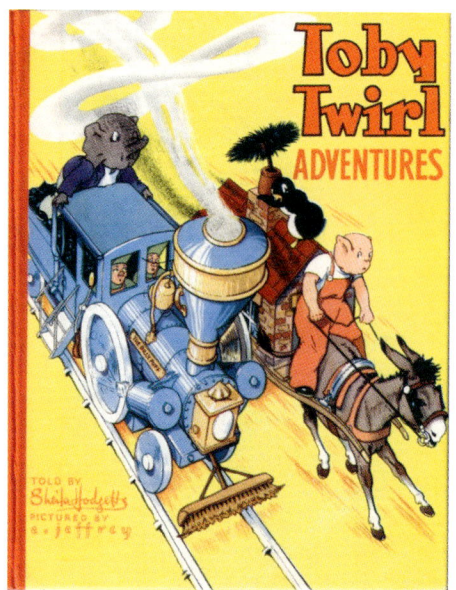

Published Price 7/6d. Thirteenth and last of the 'Annual' Toby Twirl Books. 10" x 8". 75 pages - this time again with a mixture of full colour and single colour page printing. Featuring six stories. This is the only book that does not carry the publisher name of Sampson Low and it there-fore may have been pro-duced entirely by Purnell & Sons who had previously been the printers for Sampson Low.

Contents:

Game: Let's Collect Insects with Toby
Adventures in Arabia
A Picture to Paint
Toby and Pepi the Marionette
Toby in Dillyland Again
The Dilly-Paddle's Voyage of Discovery
The Mailbag Robbery
Sweeping a Chimney
Game: The Grand Hill Climb

Value Guide £35/£40.

Above: **Sampson Low Advertisement 1947**

Above: **Sampson Low Advertisement 1948**

The Collector's Guide - Part 2

Toby Twirl

'Toby Twirl Tales' - Toby Twirl Library
Set of 8 (5 1/2" x 7 1/2") 1949 – 1954

This is a charming set of eight books and very much sought after by collectors.

Each volume features two 'Toby Twirl' stories and all were published by Sampson Low & Marston, priced 3/6d each, as part of their 'Children's Library' series; which also included a number of 'Nicholas Thomas' and Enid Blyton's 'Noddy' books.

Copies without the red number on the front, a feature of this set from book 3 onwards, are first editions; examples are only known for volumes 1 and 2, these being reprinted before the issue of book No3 to feature the distinctive red number on the front cover and bottom of the spine.

Examples are known featuring a yellow number on the spine cover and a red number on the front cover; all first editions have a rounded spine cover whilst later editions have a flat spine cover.

The following price guide is for 'Toby Twirl Tales' 'first edition' series in 'Very Good ' (VG) Condition, expect to pay at least £10 more for books with good original dust wrappers where available and £15 to £20 for books in 'Near Fine' (NF). For books in only 'Good' (G) condition deduct 50%. For books in 'Poor' (P) condition deduct 75%. *See page 56 for condition guide details.*

1949
Toby Twirl Tales No.1

Published Price 3/6d. First Edition - recognisable by the absence of the Red Series number to front board.

Stories In This Edition:
The Weeping Dragon
The Imp Of Mischief

Value Guide £40

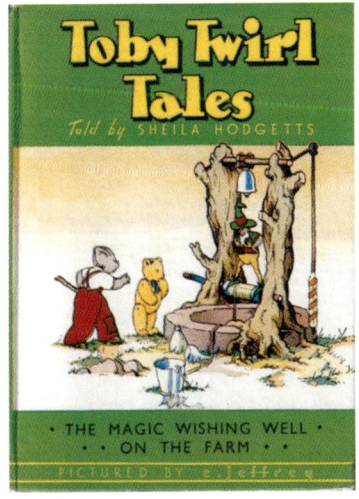

1949
Toby Twirl Tales No.2

Published Price 3/6d. First Edition - recognisable by the absence of the Red Series number to front board

Stories In This Edition:
The Magic Wishing Well
On The Farm

Value Guide £40

> **Note:** All 'Toby Twirl Tales' were published with dust wrappers that matched the books' cover boards.

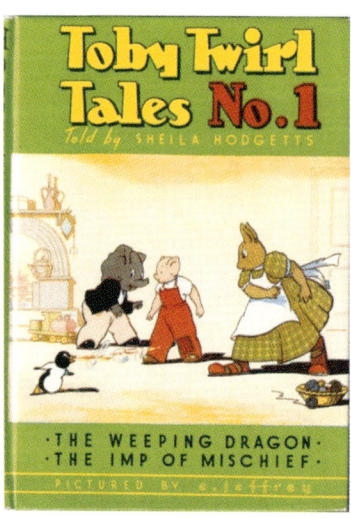

1950
Toby Twirl Tales No.1

Published Price 3/6d. Second Edition - recognisable by the Red Series number to front board.

Stories In This Edition:
The Weeping Dragon
The Imp Of Mischief

Value Guide £35

1950
Toby Twirl Tales No.2

Published Price 3/6d. Second Edition - recognisable by the Red Series number to front board.

Stories In This Edition:
The Magic Wishing Well
On The Farm

Value Guide £35

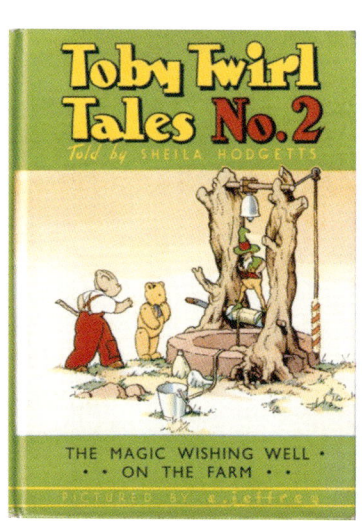

1951
Toby Twirl Tales No.3

Published Price 3/6d.

Stories In This Book:
The Roaring Donkey
The Toy Lord Mayor's Show

Value Guide £35

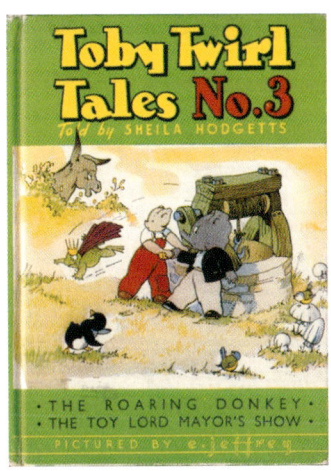

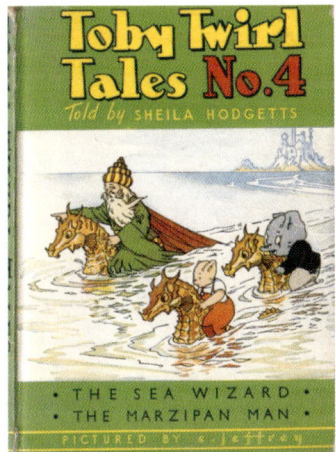

1951
Toby Twirl Tales No.4

Published Price 3/6d.

Stories In This Book:
The Sea Wizard
The Marzipan Man

Value Guide £35

1952
Toby Twirl Tales No.5

Published Price 3/6d.

Stories In This Book:
The Jumbo Giant
The Toy Soldier

Value Guide £35

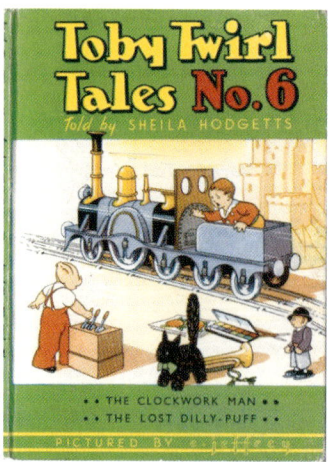

1952
Toby Twirl Tales No.6

Published Price 3/6d

Stories In This Book:
The Clockwork Man
The Lost Dilly Puff

Value Guide £35

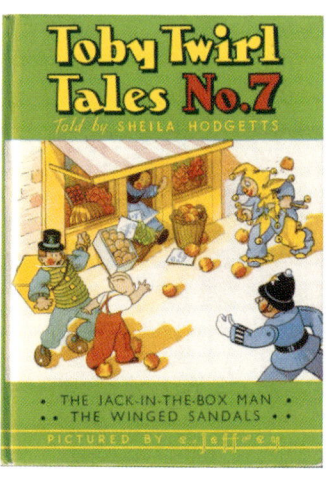

1953
Toby Twirl Tales No.7

Published Price 3/6d

Stories In This Book:
The Jack In The Box Man
The Winged Sandals
Value Guide £35

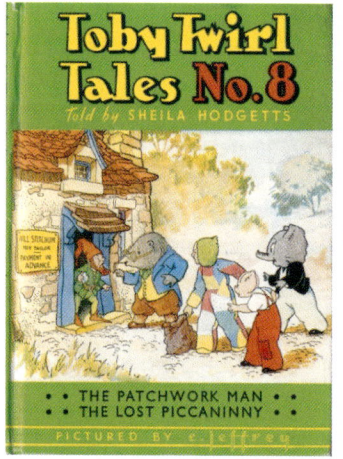

1954
Toby Twirl Tales No.8

Published Price 3/6d.

Stories In This Book:
The Patchwork Man
The Lost Piccaninny

Value Guide £35

Finding Toby Twirl - Collecting Tips

A good source for Toby Twirl books is *www.abebooks.co.uk*; this is a well-established on-line international association for book dealers and is highly recommended. Log on to above address and type in 'Toby Twirl' then click on search, wait a few moments when many Toby Twirl books could be on offer at one time from book dealers all around the world.

Another good source is *www.booksearch.com*, very similar to above.

If you enjoy bargain hunting and the thrill of an auction you could try your hand at *www.ebay.co.uk* and bid for the books, when available, or the more specialist auction site of Martin Hamer's Annual and Comic Auction House on *www.hamerbooks.co.uk* where regular auctions are held with an on-line catalogue available.

There are also a good number of specialist Children's Book Dealers, many of which advertise on the Internet and can be found by a simple search on your internet service providers search engine.

If you can't find the one you are looking for send an email to *search@tobytwirl.co.uk* and I may be able to help you, since I usually try to keep a stock of 'Toby Twirl Annuals' and 'Toby Twirl Tales' books for sale.

Other Books by Sheila Hodgetts and Illustrated by Edward Jefferey

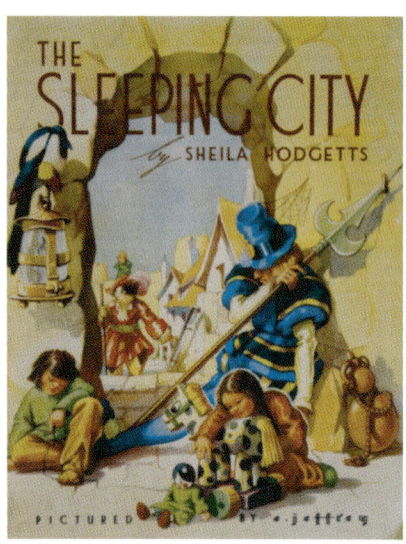

1947
The Sleeping City

Published by Sampson Low price 2/6d. Large format card cover book featuring one Story 16 colour pages. Actual Book size 14" x 9".

Value Guide £35

1947
One Magic Night

Published by Sampson Low price 2/6d. Large format card cover book featuring one Story and 16 colour pages. Actual Book size 14" x 9".

Value Guide £35

Some Other Books by Sheila Hodgetts

Book on Left:
1953

Book on Right:
1954

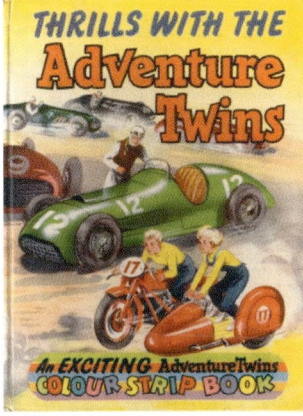

The Adventure Twins
/ Thrills With The Adventure Twins

Illustrated by R.MacGillivery. Each featuring seven Stories: Published by Sampson Low priced 4/6d.
Value Guide £25 each.

In addition to the larger hard back book, pictured right, there are a number of small card covered books by Sheila Hodgetts titled: **'Sleepy Times Tales'** (shown below) published by Sampson Low from 1951, priced 1/6d, each featuring 15 x 5 minute stories.

Value Guide £7 each

1964
'Sleepy Time Book'

Published by Purnell & Sons.
Value Guide £15.00

Collector's Book Grading Guide

Near Mint (NM) No apparent obvious defects; high cover gloss; no fading; covers flat, centred and unworn; spine flat and tight; interior pages clean and white. Permissible defects: minute page creases; small binding or printing faults, complete with any original dust wrapper.

Near Fine (NF) Several minor defects but not including completed, or partly completed, colouring or activity pages; good cover gloss; minimal surface wear; near flat cover; very minor corner, edge, or spine wear; light cover markings permitted; interior paper may be off-white.

Very Good (VG) No major defects but an accumulation of minor ones, including corner dings and normal edge wear to boards; completed, or partly completed, colouring or activity pages; minor page creases and light spine wear; interior paper may be off-white.

Good (G) Complete and readable; marked pages with heavy edge wear to boards; small pieces may be missing; interior pages may be tanned with some 'Foxing' but not brittle.

Poor (P) Curiosity value only; badly worn boards with heavy rubbing. Sometimes referred to as 'a reading copy' or 'collection completer', better than no copy at all as you can always improve your collection over a period of time.

The addition of the - or + symbol after one of the above grades, indicates a condition between, below or above that grade towards the next grade.